Woman's Workshop Series

PERFECT IN HIS EYES

STUDIES ON SELF-ESTEEM

KAY MARSHALL STROM

Lamplighter Books Grand Rapids, Michigan
Zondervan Publishing House

This is a Lamplighter Book
Published by the Zondervan Publishing House,
1415 Lake Drive, S.E., Grand Rapids, Michigan 49506

Library of Congress Cataloging in Publication Data

Strom, Kay Marshall, 1943–
  Perfect in his eyes.

  "Lamplighter books."
  1. Self-respect—Religious aspects—Christianity. 2. Women—Religious life. 3.
Women—Conduct of life. I. Title.
BV4647.S43S77   1988   248.8'43   88-68
ISBN 0-310-33691-0

All Scripture quotations, unless otherwise noted, are taken from the HOLY BIBLE:
NEW INTERNATIONAL VERSION (North American Edition). Copyright © 1973,
1978, 1984, by the International Bible Society. Used by permission of Zondervan
Bible Publishers.

Springtime in Giverny by Claude Monet
Cover Photo by SUPERSTOCK INTERNATIONAL
Cover Design by *The Church Art Works*, Salem, Oregon

Edited by Linda Vanderzalm and John Sloan

Printed in the United States of America

    90 91 92 93 94 95 96 / CH / 11 10 9 8 7 6 5 4

Books in the Woman's Workshop Series

CONTENTS

INTRODUCTION

The need to be a special person, to have personal worth is basic to each of us. Indeed, one of the most valuable possessions any of us can have is a strong, healthy self-image. Our sense of personal worth not only establishes the boundaries of our successes but also sets the limits on our accomplishments.

All of us have times when our self-esteem is low; we feel insecure, inadequate, and unhappy with ourselves. At other times our self-esteem is high; we are comfortable, self-assured, and confident. We fluctuate between relative contentment and nagging dissatisfaction. Sometimes we like ourselves; other times we don't. It is the final balance of these pluses and minuses that gives us a sense of our own value. For some it is positive. For too many it is negative.

Far from being a frivolous quest—some would go so far as to say it is downright sinful—pursuing a positive attitude toward yourself can be one of the healthiest things you can do. A strong self-image will provide you with a foundation upon which you can grow and mature into the person God wants you to be. The message of this study is that the solution to the problem of sagging self-esteem lies in understanding how precious you are to the God who created you and who desires to continue to mold you into his own likeness.

Perhaps you, like many other people, are hoping for a miracle that will help you suddenly feel happy, confident, and good about yourself. Unfortunately, it doesn't work that way. No one matures instantly—not physically, not spiritually, and not emotionally. Correcting what is wrong in your life will take time and effort.

As you progress through the thirteen lessons in this guide, be patient with yourself. Understand that growth, like change, comes slowly. Sometimes it comes painfully. But it can come.

I pray that this study will help you discover your own wonderful uniqueness through Jesus Christ, that you will be liberated to reach out in a renewed loving acceptance of others, and that you will make God's Word the living foundation stone upon which you build your perception of who you are.

HOW TO USE THIS STUDY

This study guide was designed to be used in a group setting, with the group members doing the exercises in class, not before the group meets. Each lesson consists of an opening group activity, exercises that lead to personal examination and growth, study of appropriate Bible passages, and directions for closing prayers. The interaction between group members is important in this study. And because one group activity builds on another, the lesson is best done in the group meeting.

However, if you wish to study about self-esteem on your

own, you also will find the study meaningful. You can do many of the opening exercises on your own, and nearly all of the questions can be answered without the group. In a few instances, you will want to ask for feedback or reflections from a family member or close friend. Whether you use the study guide in a group or by yourself, the Lord will use it to encourage you and teach you about your infinite worth.

1

SELF-ESTEEM: WHAT IS IT?

I. Draw a picture of yourself as you see you. Without showing your drawing to the group, write three words that summarize what you intend it to show about yourself.

On the scale below, rate the way you feel about yourself today. (Be honest.)

lowest of the	one of the nicest
low	people I know

1. What causes our feelings about ourselves to fluctuate?

_____

2. What makes us feel good about ourselves? _____

_____

_____

3. What brings down our self-esteem? _____

_____

_____

II. Your self-image isn't what you are or even what other people think you are. It's what *you think* you are. And self-esteem is feeling good or satisfied about what you think you are.

1. Our feelings about ourselves can come from many different sources. What are your feelings about yourself based on? Use the spaces below to fill in specific ideas, both positive and negative.

Parents	Other People

Physical Traits	Talents and Abilities

Successes and Failures	Other

2. In which box are your responses most positive? _____

3. In which box are they most negative? _____

No parent is perfect. And despite our best efforts, we do hurt and tear each other down. To make matters worse, we insist upon setting up unrealistic goals for ourselves. Then when we find we can't live up to our lofty expectations, we are flooded with feelings of failure and guilt. The result is that we enter adulthood totally unable to accept ourselves as we are. And we can accept ourselves only if we can live up to certain expectations and only if others are willing to accept us. Our self-esteem will remain conditional until we allow God to rebuild its faulty foundation.

III. Read Romans 12:1–21.

1. According to verse 3, followers of Christ are to evaluate themselves: (Circle the best answer)

> critically
> kindly
> honestly
> not at all

a. What does this means to you personally? _____

_____

_____

b. When is it hardest for you to see yourself honestly?

_____

_____

c. When is it easiest? _____

_____

_____

2. Feeling inadequate, whether in a specific situation or in life generally, is one of the greatest threats to your self-esteem. It's hard to feel good about yourself when it seems as if everyone else has greater gifts, talents, and abilities than you do. How could verses 4 and 5 help you arrive at a more honest view of yourself? _____

_____

_____

3. What part of the body do you think you are? Why? _____

_____

_____

4. After each statement write *agree* or *disagree:*

a. Only parts with major jobs are important to the body (not hair or toes). _____

b. Only beautiful parts are important to the body (not feet or elbows). _____

c. Only obvious parts are important (not lungs or vocal cords). _____

d. There is no such thing as an unnecessary or worthless part of the body of Christ. _____

5. Are any of us without gifts? (vv. 6–8) _____

6. Write down three gifts or abilities you have. _____

_____

_____

_____

7. How can you use those gifts and abilities for the Lord?

_____

_____

_____

8. Why do you think Paul speaks about love (v. 9–10) immediately after talking about our gifts? _____

_____

_____

9. How can expressing love affect our self-image? _____

_____

_____

10. Check those items that are true about love:

☐ Love is a complete emptying of oneself.

☐ Love springs from good will toward oneself.

☐ Every part of the body has its own way of expressing love.

☐ God is the only source of love.

11. "Love includes feelings, intentions, and actions. All of these aspects are important, but actions are the most important of all." Do you agree with this statement? Why or why not? _____

_____

_____

_____

IV. Think of someone you'd especially like to encourage and build up. List some specific ways you'll encourage that person this week. Perhaps next week you'll be willing to share with the group what you did and what effect it had on the person you selected (and on yourself as well!). _____

_____

_____

_____

God knew what he was doing when he made you the way you are. And God never makes mistakes! Instead of wishing you were different, thank God for his perfect workmanship—YOU! Let's close this first session by thanking him together.

2

BEAUTY, INTELLIGENCE, AND WEALTH

I. Cut out magazine pictures that show the type of woman who is most admired in our society. Glue the pictures to a piece of poster board to make a collage of "The Ideal American Woman."

1. Take a few minutes to examine your masterpiece. From what you see there, what characteristics does our society seem to value the most? _____

_____

_____

2. Which of these characteristics do you see in yourself?

_____

3. When we look at the eternally young and beautiful faces of these "ideal women," dressed in beautiful clothes, bedecked by lovely jewelry, driving expensive cars, living in stunning homes, and surrounded by attractive, successful families, it's easy to understand why we have trouble feeling good about ourselves. For most of us, what we see out there is not at all the image we see when we look in our mirrors!

Fill in the boxes below. You will use your answers later.

My Strongest Characteristics	My Weakest Characteristics

II. After each statement write *agree* or *disagree:*

A. Cinderella, Snow White, and Sleeping Beauty did us no favor. _____

B. There is life after 30. _____

C. You can never be too rich. _____

D. Our society sees physically attractive people as more confident, more intelligent, and more socially acceptable.

_____

E. Because femininity is closely tied to attractiveness, unattractive women carry a greater burden than unattractive men. _____

1. Look again at the above statements. With which do you agree most strongly? Explain your choice. _____

_____

_____

2. We have grown up engulfed by our society's value system, and it's being reinforced every day. Consider the following familiar statements (you may want to add a few of your own):

Advertisement: "Lose weight fast! A slimmer figure is your road to a life of happiness and success."

Parent: "You're a mess! Why can't you be like Susie? She always looks so nice!"

Teacher: "Here are the students who got A's . . ."

Television: "Live, from Atlantic City! The most beautiful woman in America!"

Friend: "Did you hear about Jessica's promotion? If I had her money, all my worries would be over!"

The obvious suggestion is that beauty, wealth, and intelligence lead to love, happiness, acceptance, and success. How strongly do you think your attitudes are affected by each of these sources of input? _____

_____

_____

III. Read 1 Samuel 16:1–13.

1. Mark the best answer to each question:

  a. Samuel's assignment was to

    _____ choose a new king.

    _____ anoint the man whom God had chosen to be king.

    _____ get to know some of the important families in Bethlehem.

  b. When he saw Eliab, Samuel thought:

    _____ *this fellow has my vote!*

    _____ *he's tall, he's strong, he's handsome. Surely he is the one God has chosen to be the next king.*

    _____ *I wonder what his heart is like?*

c. After Samuel had seen seven of Jesse's sons, Samuel said:

___ "You sure have a good-looking bunch of boys, Jesse!"

___ "Look at them again, God. Surely there is *one* you can use!"

___ "Are these all the sons you have?"

2. What do you think each of these people thought about David becoming the next king?

Samuel _____

David's seven brothers _____

Jesse _____

David _____

3. Write out a verse (or part of a verse) that addresses the issue of self-esteem. _____

_____

Is this an encouragement or a discouragement to you? Why? _____

_____

IV. Examine your own values:

1. Look back at the boxes you filled in on the first page of this lesson.

a. Of the characteristics you listed, both strengths and weaknesses, how many are related to physical attributes? ___

b. How many are related to social position, intellect, or finances? _____

c. How many are related to inward characteristics? _____

d. How many are related to your relationship to God? ___

2. After looking at your answers to the above questions, write a brief analysis of your own value system. _____

_____

_____

_____

3. What may need to be changed in your value system?

_____

Aren't you glad God disagrees with our society's value system? In his eyes every single person is valuable and infinitely worthwhile—and that includes you! David expressed it beautifully in Psalm 139. Verses 13—16 are printed below for you to read responsively. (Leader reads the verses in regular print, and the group responds with the italicized verses.)

For you created my inmost being;
you knit me together in my mother's womb.

I praise you because I am fearfully and
wonderfully made;
your works are wonderful, I know that full well.

My frame was not hidden from you
when I was made in the secret place.

When I was woven together in the depths
of the earth,
your eyes saw my unformed body.

All the days ordained for me were written
in your book
before one of them came to be.

3

THE ONLY TRUE VALUES

I. According to 1 Samuel 16:7, we look "at the outward appearance, but the Lord looks at the heart." On the outline of a person on the next page, list or draw those things you think other people look for. On the heart, list or draw those things God wants to see.

1. Put stars beside the two things you think are most important to God and the two things you think are most important to other people.

2. How do you feel you rate each of the priorities listed below? Put an X on each line to indicate your rating.

God's Priorities		Society's Priorities	
buried six feet under	top of the heap	buried six feet under	top of the heap

II. The three following statements describe the effects of basing one's sense of personal worth on outward appearances. Decide to what extent you agree or disagree with each one. Then mark your position on the line below with an *X*. Be prepared to explain your decision.

Statement 1: However hard we try to prove our worth by physical appearance, material success, intellectual performance, or social status, we inevitably fall short.

Absolutely not!   Couldn't be more right!
Disagree 100%   Agree 100%

Statement 2: Criticism and rejection are sure to follow.

Absolutely not!   Couldn't be more right!
Disagree 100%   Agree 100%

Statement 3: Guilt, fear, anxiety, and a feeling of failure creep in to undermine the sense of worthiness we are so desperately trying to build up.

Absolutely not!   Couldn't be more right!
Disagree 100%   Agree 100%

III. Read Micah 6:6–8.

1. In three short statements Micah sums up what God looks for in each of us. What specifics do you think are included in each general statement?

```
+-----------------------------+   +-----------------------------+
| ACT JUSTLY                  |   | LOVE MERCY                  |
|                             |   |                             |
|                             |   |                             |
|                             |   |                             |
|                             |   |                             |
+-----------------------------+   +-----------------------------+

        +-----------------------------+
        | WALK HUMBLY WITH            |
        | YOUR GOD                    |
        |                             |
        |                             |
        |                             |
        +-----------------------------+
```

2. Which of the following characteristics are valued by God?

☐ love for God   ☐ love for others   ☐ humble spirit

☐ obedience to   ☐ watching out for   ☐ respect for
    God   yourself   authority

☐ development of   ☐ making sure eve-   ☐ worrying about
    a personal   ryone knows you   who loves you
    relationship to   are as good as   and how much
    God   the next
                        person

3. How do you feel about this statement? Mark your position with an X.

Statement: When God's values replace the artificial and destructive ones that the world holds dear, we are able to replace hopeless frustration with the sense of worthiness that allows us to become all that he intends us to be.

Absolutely not!   Couldn't be more right!
Disagree 100%   Agree 100%

IV. What does God see when he looks at your heart? Circle where you think you stand in each area: 1 means your heart is empty of this characteristic; 10 means your heart is full. (Be as honest as you can. You won't be asked to share your answers.)

My love for God   My respect for his authority
1 2 3 4 5 6 7 8 9 10   1 2 3 4 5 6 7 8 9 10

My desire to obey him   My love for others
1 2 3 4 5 6 7 8 9 10   1 2 3 4 5 6 7 8 9 10

My true desire for honesty   The humility of my spirit
1 2 3 4 5 6 7 8 9 10   1 2 3 4 5 6 7 8 9 10

Because he sees your heart, God knows all about you—your strengths and weaknesses, your gifts and abilities, your insecurities, failings, and fears. And yet God loves you. The true basis for a healthy self-concept is an understanding and acceptance of the fact that you are loved by God, unconditionally and voluntarily, regardless of what you are or what you are not. (We'll see more about this in lesson 4.)

1. Will improving your relationship to God strengthen your sense of self-worth? Explain your answer. _____

_____

_____

2. By being involved in this study, you are taking steps toward developing a closer relationship to God. What else can you do?

_____

_____

V. Are you encouraged by the fact that God judges you on the basis of what is in your heart? Or do you worry about what he sees when he looks within you? Have you thought of things in your life that displease him? If you ask him to, he can help you change those things.

Spend some time in silent prayer discussing the secrets of your heart with the One who already knows them all. Then as a group, close with sentence prayers, asking the Lord for insight, wisdom, and help in your pursuit of becoming women after God's own heart.

4

SEEING YOURSELF THROUGH GOD'S EYES

I. Take an envelope and several blank sheets of paper. Use one sheet for each of the other members of your group and on it write the qualities you have seen and admired in each of those women. (Keep the remaining blank sheets to use later on.)

When everyone has finished writing, give each person the slip that describes her. Now take a minute to read and enjoy what the others have written about you.

1. What quality mentioned especially pleases or encourages you? _____

_____

Share it with the group if you're comfortable.

2. How do the papers you received make you feel? Check the statements that best describe your feelings.

___ flattered

___ embarrassed

___ I don't believe a word of it

___ pretty accurate observations

___ I'd rather have different qualities

Kind words from others are great, but your sense of self-esteem can't rest on their opinion alone. Only God's opinion can provide you with an absolutely sure and safe foundation on which to build.

II. How would you complete these sentences?

1. When I get a compliment, I feel _____

_____

2. When I read or sing about God's love for me, I feel ____

_____

3. When I am criticized, I feel _____

_____

4. When I do something wrong, I feel _____

_____

5. When I hear about a party to which I wasn't invited, I feel _____

_____

6. When I think about Jesus dying for me, I feel _____

_____

7. In your opinion, when God sees you through his eyes, he

☐ is sorry he made you.

☐ sees a precious creation.

☐ sees his own image.

☐ sees a sinful worm.

☐ is filled with love for you.

☐ doesn't know who you are.

III. Read Psalm 139:7–16.

1. What do you think David is saying in this Psalm?

WHEN HE SAYS: HE MEANS:

a. Even the darkness will _____
not be dark to you   _____
(v. 12)   _____

b. You knit me together in _____
my mother's womb   _____
(v. 13)   _____

c. My frame was not hid- _____
den from you (v. 15)   _____
                          _____

d. All the days ordained _____
for me were written in   _____
your book before one of   _____
them came to be   _____
(v. 16)   _____

You didn't just happen to come into being, and it wasn't chance that you are who you are. Long before you were born, you were planned in the mind of God. You are uniquely designed, a very special person, like no one else on earth.

2. From the first chapter of Genesis to the last chapter of Revelation, the Bible is filled with evidence of your importance to God. Just look at what it says:

a. You were made in God's _____ (Gen. 1:27).

b. You were not redeemed with _____ but with _____ (1 Peter 1:18).

c. God wants to give you _____ (Rom. 8:32).

d. God wants to adopt you, to make you his _____ _____ (Rom. 8:15–17).

e. He has prepared a _____ for you, and he will _____ so that _____ (John 14:2–3).

IV. There's still more! The Bible is filled to overflowing with promises from God to you.

1. Choose one of the promises listed below to claim as your own special promise. Put a check in the box beside your choice. Then memorize the verse and share it with the group next week.

☐ "Being confident of this, that he who began a good work in you will carry it on to completion until the day of Christ Jesus" (Phil. 1:6).

☐ "And God is able to make all grace abound to you, so that in all things at all times, having all that you need, you will abound in every good work" (2 Cor. 9:8).

☐ "I can do everything through him who gives me strength" (Phil. 4:13).

☐ "And we know that in all things God works for the good of those who love him, who have been called according to his purpose" (Rom. 8:28).

☐ "Who shall separate us from the love of Christ? Shall trouble or hardship or persecution or famine or nakedness or danger or sword? . . . No, in all these things we are more than conquerors through him who loved us. For I am convinced that neither death nor life, neither angels or demons, neither the present nor the future, nor any powers, neither height nor depth, nor anything else in all creation, will be able to separate us from the love of God that is in Christ Jesus our Lord" (Rom. 8:35, 37–39).

2. Now take the blank slips of paper left from the opening exercise. On each paper, write one proof of God's love for you, then put it back in the envelope with the slips your group members filled out for you. You now have a self-esteem envelope. Whenever you need to be assured of your personal value, pull out a slip of paper and read it. You are truly loved!

Because you don't feel something doesn't mean it isn't so. The reality of God's love for you, his unconditional accept-ance of you, and his desire to have you become his child has nothing to do with the way you feel. God's love for you is unchangeable. And it is unconditional.

V. What wonderful truths we have explored today—so wonderful that they are worth reviewing again and again. To help set them in your mind, read the statements below in unison:

I was made in the image of God. Sin corrupted his perfect creation, but God sent his own Son to provide a way to bring me back to him. God loves me enough to want me in his family. I am loved. I am worthwhile. No matter how I feel, I am precious in God's sight!

Spend some time praying together, thanking God for his great love for you.

5

KNOW YOURSELF

I. Have you ever played charades? If so, you know you can sometimes end up with situations that seem impossible to act out. We would like to start this session with some acting, but here you can choose your own situation to portray.

Think of a situation in which you feel pressure to act in a way that will please someone else. Tell the other group members the situation, then act out a possible way to handle it.

Example: You are given a hand-knit sweater that is poorly made and too small. You know you'll never be able to wear it, yet you feel pressure to tell the giver how beautiful the gift is and how much use you'll get from it. Act out a way to show your gratitude for the thoughtfulness of the giver, but don't be untrue to yourself.

If you can't think of times when you feel pressure to please others, think of the pressure these statements might produce in certain situations:

"Don't be angry."   "Say you're sorry."
"Don't be such a crybaby."   "Tell her how nice she looks."
"It's ridiculous to be afraid."   "You don't want to eat that!"

From childhood, most of us have been taught to hide our emotions, reactions, and true feelings. The important thing, we are told, is to keep everyone happy. In time we become so conditioned to doing this that we do nothing but act out what we think other people want to see. Of course, you don't want to cause pain or embarrassment to another person. But it is important to be honest with yourself. Trying to be what you are not tears down your self-esteem.

II. Who and what are you?

1. Read each statement below and check *TRUE* if you agree with it, *FALSE* if you don't.

TRUE   FALSE

_____ _____ I'm a sinner.
_____ _____ A stranger on the street would think I'm perfect.
_____ _____ God sees the love I have for him.
_____ _____ I was created by God in his image.
_____ _____ I have no abilities to speak of.
_____ _____ God made me the way he wants me to be.
_____ _____ I can't be satisfied with myself.
_____ _____ I want to be the person God wants me to be.

2. How would you complete these sentences?

a. The part of me for which I am most thankful is _____

b. The characteristic I would most like God to help me change is _____

c. If I were someone else meeting me for the first time, I would be most impressed by _____

_____

_____

III. Read Galatians 6:2–5.

Using the verses you just read, fill in the blanks below:

1. Carry each other's _____.

2. If you think you are _____ when you are _____, you _____ yourself.

3. Test your own _____. Then you can take _____ in yourself, without _____ yourself to somebody else.

You have just made a personalized version of these verses. Read through them silently. What do they say to you? _____

_____

_____

_____

IV. Galatians 5:22–23 talks about the "fruit of the Spirit," traits of those who belong to Christ Jesus.

1. In the boxes on the next page, list ways in which each of these fruits can be seen in you.

2. Share your ideas with the group. If other group members think of things you missed, they should feel free to add that idea into your "fruit."

Love	Joy	Peace

Patience	Kindness	Goodness

Faithfulness	Gentleness	Self-control

3. Now, as Galatians 6:4 instructs, take a moment to test yourself. Give yourself a rating from 1 to 10 in each of the following areas: 1 represents large amounts of that fruit evident in your life; 10 represents none of that fruit evident. (Be honest. You don't have to show your ratings to anyone.)

____ Love
____ Joy
____ Peace
____ Patience
____ Kindness
____ Goodness
____ Faithfulness
____ Gentleness
____ Self-control

4. Are you pleased with your scores? _____

5. In which area are you strongest? _____

6. In which do you need the most improvement? _____

V. Whatever you are—whatever your strengths, whatever your weaknesses—God can use you. But this does not mean you have to settle for what you are today. Your strengths can grow stronger, and your weaknesses can be turned into strengths.

As we close this session in prayer, take time to

- thank God for the spiritual fruits he has made available to you.
- ask him to allow these fruits to develop and mature in your life.
- dedicate yourself to the Lord—with all your strengths and weaknesses.
- thank God for his love for you.

6

BE CRITICAL, BE KIND

I. Without taking too much time to think out your answers, complete the following ten sentences. Try to be as spontaneous as possible.

1. I am _____
2. I am _____
3. I am _____
4. I am _____
5. I am _____
6. I am _____
7. I am _____
8. I am _____
9. I am _____
10. I am _____

1. How many of your responses are positive? ___ Congratulations! You are reinforcing the good in yourself.

2. How many are negative? ___ Don't let them discourage you. When you find a deficiency, you have found a new challenge, a new area for growth.

Understanding how you see yourself is an important first step. But that alone is not enough. You also need to gain insights into the ways you contribute to and perpetuate your specific problems. Only then can you take action toward finding solutions.

II. Check the answer that best describes your situation.

My family:

___ Love is an important part of our family life.

___ Love? What's that?

___ I should love my family more.

God's Word:

___ I find the Bible boring.

___ I look forward to studying God's Word.

___ I should study it more.

Prayer:

___ Talking to God is like talking to my best friend.

___ "Thank you for this food" is about my limit.

___ I should pray more.

Relationships to others:

___ I like bringing joy to others.

___ I'd like to have a friend like me.

___ I should be more thoughtful to others.

Each of the above "shoulds" is a worthy ambition. But remember not to create such a list of dos and don'ts that you can't possibly live up to them all. If you make impossible goals, you set yourself up for failure, frustration, and even more negative feelings about your worth. Do set self-improvement goals, but don't make them unrealistic.

III. Read Ruth 1:1–2:12.

1. Let's review the details of the story of Ruth, Naomi, and Boaz. Read each statement below and check *TRUE* if you agree with it, *FALSE* if you don't. (Remember to base your answers on the biblical text.)

TRUE   FALSE

_____   _____   a. Like every good love story, this one revolves around a beautiful woman and a handsome man.

_____   _____   b. Naomi is sure to cause trouble. After all, she's a mother-in-law.

_____   _____   c. Naomi had a good reason for going to live in another country.

_____   _____   d. Naomi truly cared about her daughters-in-law.

_____   _____   e. Orpah was glad to be rid of Naomi.

_____   _____   f. Ruth was determined to stick with Naomi no matter what.

_____   _____   g. Boaz had heard about Ruth.

_____   _____   h. Boaz was attracted to Ruth because of her beauty.

2. In time, Boaz married Ruth (Ruth 4). Their son, Obed, was the grandfather of David, through whose line Jesus was born. What does this say about Ruth's relationship to Jesus?

_____

IV. After reading the following questions, circle the statement that best captures your response.

1. If you were facing the same crisis that Ruth faced, would your faith hold up?

a. Yes, I've been through some pretty tough spots myself.

b. No, my faith is too feeble.

c. Ask me tomorrow.

2. If you were in Naomi's place, how would you feel toward Ruth?

a. Embarrassed because she was a foreigner.

b. Obligated to watch over her.

c. Grateful for her willingness to help.

3. If you had Boaz's money, what decisions would you make?

a. Go on a month-long shopping spree.

b. Make sure my responsibilities were taken care of.

c. Let poor people glean in my fields.

Naomi had connections and she was wise. Ruth had faith and she was willing. Boaz had resources and he was caring. By working together, each doing his or her job, God accomplished his perfect plan through their lives. Do you believe he can do the same in your life? _____

Not everyone has the same strengths. You must not condemn yourself for not being able to do everything well. Though you can, with God's help, grow and develop and improve, God can use you even with your imperfections.

Avoid making comparisons with others. You are only responsible to God for yourself.

V. We are now halfway through our study, a good time for review. Take a few minutes to evaluate your life in the areas below. Circle a number between 1 and 10 (1 means the statement is totally false; 10 means the statement is totally true).

My self-esteem doesn't depend on beauty, intelligence, or wealth.

1 2 3 4 5 6 7 8 9 10

I value in myself those characteristics that God values in me.

1 2 3 4 5 6 7 8 9 10

I can evaluate myself honestly.

1 2 3 4 5 6 7 8 9 10

God loves me!

1 2 3 4 5 6 7 8 9 10

I've done a pretty good job of coming to know myself.

1 2 3 4 5 6 7 8 9 10

God can use me, with my strengths and weaknesses, for his purposes.

1 2 3 4 5 6 7 8 9 10

VI. Life is neither all good nor all bad. Life is a combination of good and evil, successes and failures, hopes, and impossibilities. Because Christians are God's children living under his loving protection and care, they have a right to look positively at life.

To close our time together, read in unison Philippians 4:8:

> *Finally, [sisters],*
> *whatever is true,*
> *whatever is noble,*
> *whatever is right,*
> *whatever is pure,*

> *whatever is lovely,*
> *whatever is admirable—*
>
> *if anything is excellent or praiseworthy—*
> *think about such things.*

Ask God to help you to concentrate on these positive characteristics in your life.

7

IS IT REALLY OK TO LOVE MYSELF?

I. Read the following story:

Claire is a good hostess. Those who have enjoyed her parties and delicious meals claim she has a real gift. When Marian joined Claire's Bible study group and confided her anxiety about her recent move to town, Claire promptly invited Marian and her husband for dinner. Marian gratefully accepted.

When Claire told her husband about Marian, he said he was certain she was the wife of the new vice-president of the company for which he worked. Immediately Claire planned an all-out affair—lobster for dinner, chocolate mousse for dessert, a dinner party to which their most impressive friends and acquaintances would be invited.

Later when Chaire mentioned to Marian that their husbands worked together, Marian responded, "That can't be. My husband doesn't work. He was in an accident that left him . . . well . . . unemployable."

That changed everything. Claire canceled her lobster order and put away her recipe for mousse. Chicken and ice cream would be good enough, and a whole lot cheaper. Then she threw away her guest list. The two couples would dine alone. With any luck, it would be a short evening.

1. Was there anything wrong with Claire recognizing and using her ability as a hostess? _____

2. For whose good was she using it? _____

3. Which do you think best describes Claire?

    a. conceited

    b. generous

    c. selfish

    d. a smart cookie

4. If Claire had asked for your advice, what would you have said?

    a. "Save your talents and money and use them where they would really count."

    b. "Make the best of the evening with Marian and her husband."

    c. "Use your talent as a hostess to make Marian and her husband feel welcome and important."

    d. "Open a catering business."

II. It may be that the entire idea of loving yourself sounds offensive to you because you don't really understand what is involved in self-love.

1. Circle the statement that best completes the following sentence:

In my opinion, loving myself means

    a. feeling superior to other people.

    b. being self-centered and conceited.

    c. understanding that God knew what he was doing when he loved me enough to send his Son to die for me.

2. Perhaps the chart below will add to your understanding of self-love:

Self-Love Doesn't Mean	Self-Love Means
a. feeling superior to others	a. knowing how valuable I am to God
b. pride	b. acknowledging both my strengths and weaknesses
c. arrogance	c. believing I was created by God and redeemed by Christ
d. selfishness	d. being able to focus on others rather than worry about how I'm measuring up
e. considering my abilities as gifts to be used by me, for me	e. looking for ways to use my gifts for the good of others

3. Do you agree with the points made on the chart? Why or why not? _____

_____

_____

4. Which point do you find most surprising? _____

_____

5. Which means the most to you personally? _____

_____

III. Read Mark 12:28–34.

1. In what four ways are you to love the Lord? _____

_____

2. What does each of these mean?

With all your _____ means _____

With all your _____ means _____

With all your _____ means _____

With all your _____ means _____

3. What is the yardstick by which you are to measure your love for your neighbor? _____

_____

IV. What does it mean to love your neighbor as yourself? (Check as many as you think apply)

☐ It's OK to be self-centered.

☐ Healthy self-esteem is important.

☐ If you don't think much of yourself, you won't think much of your neighbor either.

☐ When God made you, he liked what he saw.

☐ The way you treat others shows what you think of yourself.

☐ You won't love others if you don't love yourself.

☐ Your love for God is the basis of love in your life.

☐ No one else is as important as you are.

1. Jesus sums up all the commandments in two basic relationships. What are they?

RELATIONSHIP I	RELATIONSHIP II

2. What do you think this says about self-love? _____

_____

The command to love your neighbor, given repeatedly throughout the Bible, always also refers to loving yourself. You can't hate yourself and love others, for self-love is the foundation upon which your love for others is built.

V. You can't love others when you need them to keep proving that you are an important person. When you understand your importance to God, you will no longer need to continue verifying your worth. It is then that you will be free to love others unconditionally. A good self-concept comes from a healthy self-love and leads to an unconditional love for others. It really is OK to love yourself!

Think of other words of praise or thanksgiving to add to the prayer chain on the next page. Then close with a prayer taken from your prayer chain. (Choose one or more words from each circle.)

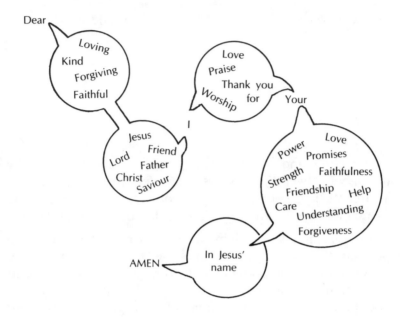

8

SINFUL PRIDE OR CHRISTIAN HUMILITY?

I. Imagine that two new poeple will join your study group. You know nothing about them except their names: Holly Humble and Patricia Proud. You probably have some instant ideas of what these two are like! Flip through a few magazines and tear out pictures that fit the image you have of the new members. Attach your pictures to the paper provided, one for Holly, the other for Patricia. You may want to add some words or captions as well.

1. What are the basic traits your group attributed to Holly Humble? _____

_____

2. What are the basic traits attributed to Patricia Proud? ___

_____

3. Which of the two would you most like to have living next door to you? Why? _____

Many people confuse self-love with pride and humility with inferiority. To them, humility means considering themselves less valuable, capable, or worthwhile than others. They are mistaken.

II. The idea of thinking so much about myself so affirmatively

- ☐ strikes fear into my heart.
- ☐ sounds okay to me.
- ☐ means I'm committing the sin of pride.
- ☐ is wrong because Christians are to be humble.
- ☐ is vaguely uncomfortable to me.
- ☐ makes me feel better about myself.
- ☐ is an idea I would like to share.

1. If you were Noah Webster working on your first dictionary, how would you define humility? _____

_____

2. How would you define self-love? _____

_____

Next to love, humility probably stands out more clearly than any other virtue in the Bible. The Greek philosophers didn't think much of it, though. And today most people in the limelight—musicians, actors, athletes, and politicians—don't seem particularly impressed with the virtue either.

III. Read Philippians 2:5–11.

1. According to Paul, Christ is to be our example of humility. With which of the following statements about

Christ do you agree? (In each blank write either *agree* or *disagree*.)

CHRIST . . .

_____ had a high position with God.

_____ talked about being inferior.

_____ took a position low in status but high in worth.

_____ was obedient even to death.

_____ was uncertain of his value as a person.

_____ was exalted after his death.

_____ needed to flaunt his strengths.

2. Do you think humility and fame or great success can ever mix? (You may also want to look at James 4:10.) _____

When Paul told us to consider others better than ourselves (Phil. 2:3), he was not suggesting that we are to feel inferior, but was saying that as secure people, we are to focus on the needs of others and how we can help them.

IV. On the chart below, check those characteristics that are true of each. You also might want to jot down comments to discuss with the group.

	Christ	Followers of Christ	Me	Comments
is proud				
focuses on success				
feels inferior				

	Christ	Followers of Christ	Me	Comments
needs to advertise strengths				
underestimates self				
overestimates self				
focuses on weakness				
focuses on abilities				
recognizes need of God				
is willing to use abilities to help others				
displays false humility				
submits to God's will				
demands respect				
does things God's way				
does what seems right in own eyes				

	Christ	Followers of Christ	Me	Comments
demands rights				
gives up rights for higher cause				
is willing to be trampled by others				
is a person of principle				
is weak				
loves others as self				
is conceited				
hates self				
respects self				
is passive				
is strong				
elevates self above others				
places self below others				

1. In one sentence summarize the characteristics of

Christ _____

Followers of Christ _____

Yourself _____

2. Share with the group any comments you made.

V. If you were to measure yourself by the yardstick of Paul's definition of humility, how would you measure up? (Check one.)

____ I would be ten feet tall.

____ I would be on the short end of the stick.

____ I would be doing all right and still growing.

____ I'm not sure.

____ Ask me tomorrow.

VI. Put an X on the line below to indicate how closely you are willing to pattern yourself after the example of Christ.

_____

I'm not sure the pattern is   I'm with him all the way
right for me

Close this session by asking the Lord to help you be more like him.

9

GET RID OF YOUR GUILT

I. Read the following skits. On the lines below each one, write out your reaction.

TO SEE OR NOT TO SEE

Linda: You went to see that movie? From what I've heard, it should have an X rating!

Kris: It wasn't that bad.

Linda: That's not what the reviewers said.

Kris: It was a contemporary story of an authentic, mature, love relationship.

Linda: Do you really believe that?

Kris: Don't be so old-fashioned. People are more open and honest now than they used to be. I think it's healthy.

_____

_____

_____

IT'S NOT MY FAULT!

Dana: I can't believe you told everyone about the problems Roger and I are having! I told you that in confidence.

Jan: You make it sound like I was gossiping.

Dana: You were! I'm so embarrassed, I can't look anyone in the eye.

Jan: Dana, it was a prayer circle. Everyone was sharing prayer requests. You asked me to pray for you, didn't you?

Dana: Just you. Not everyone.

Jan: I thought it was something the whole group should pray about.

Dana: You didn't have to go into such detail.

Jan: Those people care about you, Dana. They had a right to know what they were praying about.

_____

_____

_____

1. Which do you think best describes how Kris felt? (Mark as many as you think apply.)

____ defensive

____ guilty

____ justified

____ ready to find a new friend

2. How would you feel if you were Kris? _____

_____

_____

3. Which do you think best describes how Jan felt? (Mark as many as you think apply.)

___ defensive

___ guilty

___ justified

___ in need of a new prayer group

4. Do you think Jan did the right thing? Why or why not?

_____

II. Complete the following sentences:

1. Guilt means _____

_____

2. Guilt is good when _____

_____

3. Guilt is bad when _____

When guilt points out what is wrong in our lives so that we can correct it, it can be a healing emotion. But too often guilt doesn't stop there. It goes on to condemn us for being bad people. Even after correcting the bad deed, we find it extremely difficult to overcome those feelings of being wicked and deserving of punishment. Is guilt over some past deed holding you back? If so, keep reading. There's good news ahead!

III. Read Romans 8:1–11.

These eleven verses have a lot to say about the person who has accepted Christ's payment for sins—and a lot to say about the predicament of those who have not! In the left box, list the phrases that talk about Christians. In the right box, list phrases that refer to non-Christians.

CHRISTIANS	NON-CHRISTIANS

In which category are you? The choice is yours!

IV. Human logic doesn't always agree with what we read in God's Word. For instance:

THE BIBLE SAYS	HUMAN LOGIC SAYS
There is now no condemnation for those who are in Christ Jesus (Rom. 8:1).	You are terrible.
As far as the east is from the west, so far has he removed our transgressions from us (Ps. 103:12).	You're still guilty. Nothing can change what you've done.
Jesus Christ . . . gave himself for us to redeem us from all wickedness (Titus 2:13–14).	You must keep on paying for your sins.

1. What will you believe, the Bible or human logic? What do these verses mean to you personally? _____

_____

_____

2. Look at the statements on the next page. Next to each one check *agree* or *disagree*.

	Agree	Dis-agree
a. God doesn't care if I sin.	___	___
b. God no longer holds my sins against me.	___	___
c. Some of my sins are unforgivable.	___	___
d. God can forgive my sins.	___	___
e. I have received God's forgiveness.	___	___
f. I can regard myself as guiltless.	___	___
g. Freedom from guilt means I can go on sinning.	___	___

Guilt and fear of punishment are not appropriate for those who have accepted God's free gift of forgiveness. When Christ died on the cross, he paid the full penalty for all of our sins—past, present, and future. If you have accepted God's gift of salvation, the problem of your guilt was settled once and for all on Calvary's Cross.

V. It isn't easy to break the long-established habit of condemning yourself. But by acknowledging and accepting the fact that your sins have already been taken care of, you can begin today to grow into a fuller experience of God's forgiveness.

Let's join together in a time of guided silent prayer:

Thank you Lord for . . .

I ask your forgiveness for . . .

Because you have forgiven me, I want to forgive (name).

Thank you Lord! Amen

You are loved! You are forgiven! You are a person of infinite worth! Praise the Lord! Let's close this session by reading in unison Romans 8:31–39:

What, then, shall we say in response to this? If God is for us, who can be against us? He who did not spare his own Son, but gave him up for us all—how will he not also, along with him, graciously give us all things? Who will bring any charge against those whom God has chosen? It is God who justifies. Who is he that condemns? Christ Jesus, who died—more than that, who was raised to life—is at the right hand of God and is also interceding for us. Who shall separate us from the love of Christ? Shall trouble or hardship or persecution or famine or nakedness or danger or sword? As it is written: "For your sake we face death all day long; we are considered as sheep to be slaughtered." No, in all these things we are more than conquerors through him who loved us. For I am convinced that neither death nor life, neither angels nor demons, neither the present nor the future, nor any powers, neither height nor depth, nor anything else in all creation, will be able to separate us from the love of God that is in Christ Jesus our Lord.

10

GOD HAS GREAT PLANS FOR YOU

I. Let's begin this session by playing "Would You Rather?" Be ready to do some moving! First divide the room in half, side A and side B. The leader will read out two options: if you would prefer the first option, move to side A; if you would prefer the second, move to side B. You may have to switch after each choice.

WOULD YOU RATHER . . .

get a new pet?	get rid of the one you have?
get involved in a project?	advise others on how to do it?
have a backyard barbecue?	have dinner in a restaurant?
save for the future?	enjoy what you have now?
socialize on weekends?	relax at home on weekends?

obey God unquestioningly?   try to get God to see the situation from your point of view?

take a risk by stepping out and using your abilities?   stay in the background and support others whom you're certain could do a better job?

Every day, in every area of our lives, we have to make decisions. Some come easily, others cause us great agony. Some are merely a matter of personal preference, others deal in absolutes. Some come directly from God himself.

II. When it comes to specific situations, how would you rate yourself? Indicate your response to the following "test cases," by putting an *X* on the line somewhere between *falling apart* and *all together.*

MONEY: Handling it efficiently

_____

falling apart   all together

JOB: Finding one and being successful in it

_____

falling apart   all together

FAMILY: Seeing them through God's eyes

_____

falling apart   all together

FRIENDS: Seeing them through God's eyes

_____

falling apart   all together

OTHERS: Loving them with God's love

_____

falling apart   all together

MYSELF: Measuring my worth with God's yardstick

---

falling apart   all together

ABILITIES: Knowing what mine are

---

falling apart   all together

ABILITIES: Using mine for the good of others

---

falling apart   all together

FUTURE: Understanding what God is preparing me for

---

falling apart   all together

GOD'S WILL: Knowing it and doing it

---

falling apart   all together

God has given you gifts and abilities, and he has given you the power to use them. Whatever it is God wants you to do, you can do it!

III. Read Exodus 3:1–20 and 4:10–13.

Circle the answer that best completes these statements:

1. Moses was amazed to see the bush

    a. on fire.

    b. growing in the desert.

    c. on fire but not burning up.

2. God told Moses not to come any closer because

    a. he might get burned.

    b. he was on holy ground.

    c. he didn't have a fire extinguisher.

3. God told Moses to

    a. go to Pharaoh and lead the Israelites out of Egypt.

    b. have the Israelites elect a leader.

    c. start an underground anti-Egyptian movement.

4. As for convincing the Egyptians,

    a. God would leave that up to Moses.

    b. the Israelites would pray for him.

    c. God would take care of it.

5. When Moses said he was not a gifted speaker, God said

    a. in that case he would choose someone more qualified.

    b. Moses had better learn, and fast.

    c. he would help Moses speak and would teach him what to say.

IV. Have you ever felt as if you were expected to face mighty Pharaoh with the news that his free labor source was leaving? Well, maybe not Pharaoh exactly, but God does call us to jobs that are far beyond our natural abilities. He doesn't do this to make us feel inadequate; he does it to show that we are not bound by our natural abilities because we have access to his supernatural power. Philippians 4:13 says: "I can do everything through him who gives me strength."

1. How do you think Moses felt as he stood before the burning bush? (Check as many as apply.)

___ excited	___ terrified
___ confident	___ weak
___ unable to believe it	___ completely mystified

____ like running away   ____ able to do anything
____ strong in the Lord   ____ confused

2. How do you feel when you are faced with a job that seems far too big and impossible for you? (You may want to check more than one.)

____ excited   ____ terrified
____ confident   ____ weak
____ unable to believe it   ____ completely mystified
____ like running away   ____ able to do anything
____ strong in the Lord   ____ confused

God's methods have not changed. No matter how you feel about the job you're facing, if God has called you to do it, you need only let him take charge, and you'll find that your assets are limitless. There is nothing that you and God together can't do!

V. In the space below, write a short statement or a few phrases telling what you feel it is that God wants you to do.

_____

_____

_____

Share your statement with the others in the group. After everyone who wants to share has had a chance to do so, spend some time in prayer, thanking God for the unlimited strength he has made available to you. Then ask him for the strength to do the special job he has for you.

11

SELF-LOVE SURRENDERED

I. You're now beginning your eleventh session together as a group. During this time you've shared frustrations, hopes, goals, and prayers. You've gotten to know each other in a special way. Take a few minutes to share what the others in your group have meant to you.

As you think of each group member, concentrate on those things you especially appreciate or admire in her. Write down one or two phrases that best describe your feelings about each person.

When everyone has finished writing, throw an appreciation party. Focus on one person at a time, asking that woman to say nothing while the rest of you share what you have written about her. (Your thoughts need not be deep or profound. Such ideas as "Cathy is always willing to share" or "Susan is so honest in her responses" will allow others to see that special attribute you appreciate in the woman being honored.)

When it's your turn, sit back and listen to the words of appreciation others have for you. Enjoy it. You deserve it!

II. God loves you. And he wants you to love yourself. But he also wants you to move beyond that self-love. He wants to use your self-love as a basis for helping you love others. If you are to grow into the person he wants you to be, you need to develop meaningful relationships with others. You need the love and trust of others, and you in turn need to love, trust, and share with them.

1. When you surrender your self-love to God, amazing things will happen. Check those statements that describe what you think will happen when you surrender your self-love to God.

_____ I will submit to the lordship of Christ.

_____ I will enjoy my gifts and abilities.

_____ I will obey the Lord's commands.

_____ I will love those around me.

_____ I will want to grow spiritually.

_____ I will want to care for my physical and emotional self.

_____ I will want to help others feel good about themselves.

_____ I will be willing to accept others as they are.

2. Which items seem especially important to you? Why?

_____

_____

_____

3. Which items would you most like to see in your life? ____

_____

_____

_____

III. Read 1 John 4:10–12 and 19–21.

IN VERSE   LOVE MEANS

10   _____

11   _____

20   _____

21   _____

1. In these verses John describes two love relationships. What are they?

LOVE RELATIONSHIP I	LOVE RELATIONSHIP II

2. What does this mean? (Check all responses you consider correct.)

☐ God won't love me if I don't love others.

☐ God already loves me.

☐ Jesus died to atone for my sins.

☐ I should treat others as they treat me.

☐ God's love is complete in me.

☐ I love because God first loved me.

☐ I can't help but hate some people.

☐ I have to love only my natural-born brothers and sisters.

☐ If I love God, I will love others.

☐ If I love only myself, it will show in the way I relate to others.

IV. Love begets love. First, God loved you. Second, because of his love, you know your worth and can love yourself. Third, as a demonstration of the love you have received, you can love others.

1. Fill in the boxes below with words and phrases that describe the characteristics of these three dimensions of love.

```
┌─────────────────────────────┐
│ GOD'S LOVE                  │
│                             │
│                             │
│                             │
│                             │
└─────────────────────────────┘
```

```
┌──────────────────┐   ┌──────────────────┐
│ SELF-LOVE        │   │ LOVE FOR OTHERS  │
│                  │   │                  │
│                  │   │                  │
│                  │   │                  │
└──────────────────┘   └──────────────────┘
```

2. Loving isn't always easy. Complete these statements:

a. How can I love God when I am ill and am not being healed? _____

_____

_____

b. How can I love an abusive or violent family member?

_____

_____

c. How can I love a friend who has taken advantage of me? _____

_____

_____

d. How can I love a needy person I have never met? ____

_____

_____

We aren't meant to focus our lives on satisfying ourselves. God wants us to become more and more like Jesus Christ (Rom. 8:29). Through us, he wants the world to see what Jesus is like (2 Cor. 4:11).

V. It's hard to think of loving everyone. But it's easier when we think of beginning with the people around us. A family love tree appears on the next page. Fill in the spaces with the names of people—both in your own family and in the larger human family—to whom you will demonstrate God's love this week.

As you close this session with prayer, ask the Lord to guide you and others in your group as you seek to show love to those whose names you have recorded on your family love tree.

12

A HEALTHY SELF-CONCEPT AT WORK

I. Start this session with a game of "Give Away." Your leader will give each of you four stickers or pieces of candy. Each person in turn will roll a die, match the number rolled with the number on the chart below, and follow the instructions that correspond to the number on the die. The game is over when one player runs out of stickers or candy.

GIVE AWAY CHART	
1. Give one to the person on your left.	4. Give one to whomever you choose.
2. Give one to the person on your right.	5. Ask someone to give one to the person across from you.
3. Take one from the person who has the least.	6. Take one from or give one to whomever you choose.

1. Was it easier to give or to take? _____

_____

2. How did it feel to give to someone who was almost out?

_____

3. How did it feel to take from a person who had only a few left? _____

Relating to other people involves giving. But it is only when you have a healthy sense of your own worth that you have something to give.

II. If we concentrated on our own personal need for self-worth and failed to reach out to others, all of our relationships would become hopelessly self-centered. But in recognizing each other's worth and by serving each other in love, we are obeying the apostle Paul's admonition to "honor one another above [ourselves]" (Rom. 12:10).

Look at the heading on each box below. Then look at the verse bank. Copy each verse reference into the box(es) in which it belongs.

FORGIVING OTHERS	SHOWING GENEROSITY

HONORING OTHERS	BEING GRATEFUL

VERSE BANK

1. How long will mockers delight in mockery? (Prov. 1:22).
2. [Forgive] each other, just as in Christ God forgave you (Eph. 4:32b).
3. Give thanks in all circumstances (1 Thess. 5:18).
4. Rid yourselves of all malice (1 Peter 2:1).
5. Be kind and compassionate to one another (Eph. 4:32a).
6. In your anger, do not sin (Eph. 4:26).
7. Look after orphans and widows in their distress (James 1:27).
8. Submit to one another out of reverence for Christ (Eph. 5:21).
9. Thanks be to God for his indescribable gift (2 Cor. 9:15).
10. Honor one another above yourselves (Rom. 12:10).
11. Keep your lives free from the love of money (Heb. 13:5).
12. Do not take revenge (Rom. 12:19).
13. Whoever loves God must also love his brother (1 John 4:21).
14. Give and it will be given to you (Luke 6:38).
15. Be thankful (Col. 3:15).
16. It is more blessed to give than to receive (Acts 20:35).
17. God . . . works in you (Phil. 2:13).
18. God loves a cheerful giver (2 Cor. 9:7).

III. Read 1 Corinthians 12:1, 4–11.

In addition to the general assignment to demonstrate Jesus in your life, God has given you a specific job, and with it, special gifts to help you accomplish that job.

1. What gifts are listed in these verses? _____

_____

_____

_____

2. Which gift is most important? _____

3. Who gives the gifts? _____

4. Who receives the gifts? _____

5. Why did Paul give this information to the Corinthians? (Circle one.)

    a. to make them jealous of each other

    b. to encourage them to pray for a gift

    c. so that they would not be ignorant of the gifts they had been given

6. How willing are you to use your gifts for the good of others? (Put an *X* on the line to indicate your answer.)

_____

Forget it   There's no stopping me

The Holy Spirit gives us gifts for one purpose: so we can build up each other in the body of Christ. The gifts are intended not for our own enjoyment but to enable us to help each other.

IV. How are we willing to use our gifts?

1. Put an *X* in the box by each of the following gifts you would like to have others use to help you right now.

☐ teaching   ☐ faith   ☐ wisdom
☐ healing   ☐ other_____

2. You have a special gift that makes you indispensable to the body of Christ! How does this make you feel?

☐ ecstatic   ☐ scared   ☐ bewildered
☐ doubtful   ☐ thankful   ☐ responsible

3. How can you use your gift? _____

_____

Although your spiritual gifts are for the building up of the body of Christ, your work doesn't stop there. Unbelievers also need to see Jesus' love and kindness through you.

V. When your healthy self-image is at work, you will want to help boost the self-image of others. Below are some of the ways you can do this:

1. Offer support.

2. Emphasize the positive.

3. Try to understand the other person's point of view. Only when you have done this have you earned the right to gently and lovingly suggest a change in behavior.

4. Listen to the other person. Take the person seriously.

5. Be patient.

6. Pray for guidance. Ask the Lord to allow you to use your spiritual gifts to help the other person.

7. Pray with the person for God's healing of the scars he or she bears from past injuries in life.

8. Don't push yourself on the other person. Continue to love and support him or her, and pray for the right words at the right time.

Whom do you know who needs to learn to love and respect himself or herself? (Write that person's initials.) _____

Set aside a few minutes each day to pray for this person.

Close with a time of prayer, asking God to guide you in helping to build up the person you indicated.

13

LOOKING TOWARD YOUR ULTIMATE SELF

I. Congratulations! You have done a lot in these thirteen sessions together. In the circles on the next page, record in words, phrases, pictures, or Bible verses some of the things you have gained from this study.

1. Put a star by the one thing in each circle that means the most to you.

2. Share your starred responses with the group.

II. You are a person in the process of *becoming*. You've learned and you've grown. Yet the best is still to come. Ultimately you will be a fully mature, perfect, complete person.

1. Complete the following sentences by checking the best ending.

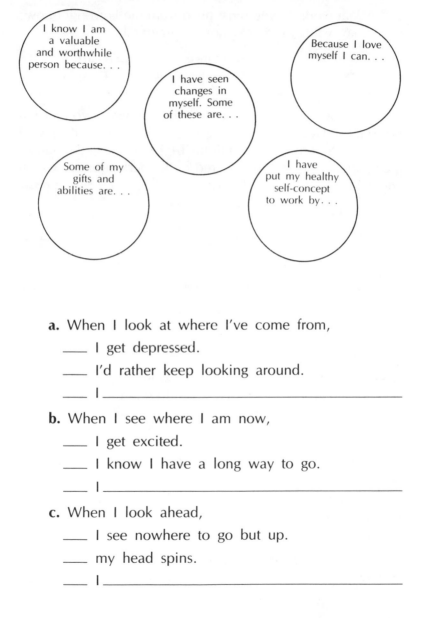

a. When I look at where I've come from,

___ I get depressed.

___ I'd rather keep looking around.

___ I _____

b. When I see where I am now,

___ I get excited.

___ I know I have a long way to go.

___ I _____

c. When I look ahead,

___ I see nowhere to go but up.

___ my head spins.

___ I _____

2. What work do you most need from the Lord right now? (You may want to check more than one.)

___ Forgiveness	___ Assurance	___ Peace
___ Hope	___ Encouragement	___ Patience
___ Other_____		

According to the Bible, you will live forever. If you have a personal relationship with Jesus Christ, you will spend eternity with him in heaven (John 14:1–3). Created in God's image, you will then be restored to the perfection for which you were originally intended.

III. Read 1 John 3:1–3.

1. Because God loves us so much, he calls us _____

_____

2. The reason the world does not know us is that _____

_____

3. When Christ returns, we will _____, for we shall _____

4. Regardless of how wonderful it is to be assured you are special and worthwhile now, it can't be compared with the joys you will know when _____

_____

5. Many portions of Scripture, including the entire book of Revelation, speak of the glorious future to which you can look forward. If you have placed your faith in Christ, these promises are for you:

- Your body will become like his (Phil. 3:21).
- You will bear the likeness of God (1 Cor. 15:49).
- Jesus has prepared a special place for you (John 14:2).

• You will spend a wonderful eternity with God (Rev. 22:1–5).

6. What does each of these promises mean to you?

A body like Christ's	Bearing the likeness of Christ
A place prepared for you	An eternity with God

IV. How do you think the Christians who first read John's letter felt about John's words? (Check as many as you want.)

____ depressed	____ encouraged	____ mystified
____ excited	____ skeptical	____ confused
____ relieved	____ hopeful	____ frightened

1. How do you feel about John's words? (Check as many as you want.)

____ encouraged	____ mystified	____ excited
____ confused	____ can't believe it	____ relieved
____ scared	____ filled with hope	____ I'm not sure

2. Will you be living forever with the Lord? (Check one.)

____ No.

____ I hope so.

____ I think I need to know more.

____ Absolutely!

V. As we close our last session together, take a few minutes to evaluate your own life in the areas below. For each statement, circle a number between 1 and 10 (1 means you're not doing well in that area; 10 means you're doing well in that area).

LOVING GOD

1 2 3 4 5 6 7 8 9 10

LOVING OTHERS

1 2 3 4 5 6 7 8 9 10

ACCEPTING GOD'S FORGIVENESS

1 2 3 4 5 6 7 8 9 10

SEEING MYSELF REALISTICALLY

1 2 3 4 5 6 7 8 9 10

IDENTIFYING MY GIFTS

1 2 3 4 5 6 7 8 9 10

UNDERSTANDING GOD'S WILL FOR ME

1 2 3 4 5 6 7 8 9 10

CHANGING MY VALUE SYSTEM

1 2 3 4 5 6 7 8 9 10

SEEING MYSELF THROUGH GOD'S EYES

1 2 3 4 5 6 7 8 9 10

UNDERSTANDING HOW GOD SEES ME

1 2 3 4 5 6 7 8 9 10

HANDLING MY GUILT FEELINGS

1 2 3 4 5 6 7 8 9 10

USING MY GIFTS FOR THE GOOD OF OTHERS

1 2 3 4 5 6 7 8 9 10

THANKING GOD FOR WHO I AM

1 2 3 4 5 6 7 8 9 10

Just imagine! The time is coming when you'll be perfect in the Lord. The fact that you're not perfect now doesn't affect God's love for you, and it doesn't affect your ultimate destiny. He has prepared a wonderful place for you to live with him forever. Knowing that you are of utmost importance to the God of the universe, how can you help but feel valuable and worthwhile? And how can you help but love and worship the One whose love made it all possible?

Together with the other members of your group, close with a time of thanksgiving to the Lord for his love for you and for the assurance you have of an eternity with him.

STEPS FOR ATTAINING HEALTHY
SELF-ESTEEM

1. Allow yourself to love yourself.
2. Instead of comparing yourself to others, try to be the person God intended you to be.
3. Look at yourself honestly. Assess your strengths as well as your weaknesses.
4. Don't condemn yourself. Accept God's forgiveness, forgive yourself, then go on.
5. Have an attitude of love and forgiveness toward others.
6. Do things that will make you like yourself more.
7. Choose realistic goals.
8. Seek God's praise—not the praise of others—for what you do.
9. Determine to use your abilities and gifts for the building up of others.

10. Seek out friends who will build you up, not tear you down.
11. Build up those around you.
12. Trust God to mold you into the person he wants you to be.
13. Thank God for his endless, limitless love for you.
14. Thank God for the future he has prepared for you.

HELPS FOR LEADERS

PREPARING TO LEAD

As in any discussion study, your role as leader is a most important one. You may be glad to know that you need not be a teacher. Your task is to encourage the group to discuss, discover, and share. The following suggestions are intended to assist you in accomplishing this task.

1. Pray. Spend time alone in prayer. Ask the Lord to equip you to lead this study. Trust him to lead in the life and development of each group member.

2. Study. Go through the lesson ahead of time, studying the passages, the exercises in the lessons, and the leader's helps for each lesson. (When questions ask for opinions, the answers in the helps section should be seen as suggestions, not definitive answers.) Allow the Lord to speak to you through the lesson so that you'll know where to guide the group. Assess how much time you'll want the group to spend on each section of the lesson.

3. Gather materials. Get ready any materials needed for the day's lesson. Some activities require old magazines, paper and pens, or some other items that may need to be gathered beforehand. The leader's helps will indicate what special materials are needed.

LEADING THE GROUP

1. Pray. Open each session with prayer, asking God to speak to each woman during the study time.

2. Getting started. Each lesson begins with a group activity intended to immediately involve the group members in the specific topic studied in that lesson. Help the group be creative in using that initial activity, but keep an eye on the clock so that this activity doesn't take too much of the group's time.

3. Provide an atmosphere of acceptance. Discussing personal experiences and deep feelings—especially emotionally painful ones—can be difficult for some group members. While you don't want to leave anyone out of the discussion, you do want to be careful not to prod a reluctant member into sharing more than she wants to share. You can make it easier for the women to share by providing an accepting, non-judgmental atmosphere in which all ideas have value. For questions that require personal responses, ask for volunteers or skip the sharing altogether if you feel your group isn't ready for it.

4. Read the Scripture passage aloud. You may want to ask each person to read one verse, or, especially when the passage is short, you may ask one or two people to read the entire passage. Note that I used the New International Version of the Bible in preparing these lessons. If you or your group members use another version, you'll find the wording of questions/answers to be somewhat different.

5. Keep the discussion on track. In this kind of study, it's easy to get off the subject and into sideline stories and experiences. If someone starts to discuss mistakes her parents made in raising her and you sense the discussion is moving far from the subject, listen for a short while, then gently move the group back to the exercise or passage.

6. Keep the discussion moving. Try to cover all the material in each lesson. However, be flexible. Sometimes it may be necessary to take time out to encourage or affirm one specific member.

7. Be flexible in your approach to each exercise. Some questions will lend themselves to sharing around the group circle. For others, one or two answers will be sufficient. Still others lend themselves to observations from several members with differing points of view.

8. Pray. End each session with prayer, helping the women respond to what they have learned in the study time.

May the Lord bless you as you guide your group members in their search for a healthy view of their infinite value.

1 / SELF-ESTEEM: WHAT IS IT?

I. Each student will need a piece of paper and a pencil for her drawing. Stress that this is not an art competition—stick figures are fine. Encourage all women to participate by reassuring the women that they won't have to share their work. When they have finished their drawings, remind them to summarize in three words what they intended to show about themselves, then to rate their feelings on the scale.

1. We tend to feel about ourselves the way we think other people feel about us. We have a picture of ourselves in our mind, and that picture is reinforced by the many messages we receive from others. This picture of how we see ourselves is our "self-image"; feeling good or satisfied with what we see is what we refer to as "self-esteem."

All of us have mixed feelings about ourselves. Sometimes and in some situations, we feel quite comfortable with who we are—we have high self-esteem; other times we're not at all pleased—our self-esteem is low. Comments from other people, our successes and failures, our moods—these and other things can cause our feelings about ourselves to fluctuate.

2. True praise (not empty, meaningless flattery), success, appreciation for our abilities, a secure and loving childhood, acceptance by our peers—all these help to make us feel good about ourselves.

3. Influences that are opposite of the ones mentioned in the previous answer bring down our self-esteem. We also hurt ourselves by setting up unrealistic goals. When we are unable to live up to these impossible goals, we're flooded with feelings of failure and defeat.

II. Encourage each group member to share some part of her chart. Remember to include both positive and negative influences.

III. Recognizing the basis of our self-concept can help us put negative feelings back into perspective. It's not unusual for a person to blame other people, childhood experiences, physical traits, or some personal failing for her inability to love herself. If someone in your group insists on blaming a particular circumstance or person for her problems, you may want to stress the importance of a forgiving attitude (Eph. 4:31-32). Forgiving those who have caused us hurt and damage is the first step toward our own healing.

1. Followers of Christ are to evaluate themselves honestly. Ask women to share what they think it means to be honest in evaluating oneself. Share opinions about when that honesty is hardest or easiest.

2. Romans 12:4–5 likens Christians to parts of a body, each part having a different function yet vitally important to the body as a whole. If any part is missing, the body isn't complete. This idea is beautifully amplified in 1 Corinthians 12:12–27.

3. Allow each group member to share her idea.

4. The only true statement is *d*. Some parts of the body are more beautiful that others, some more prominent, some more readily praised, but *all* are important. If any one part is missing, the body is incomplete and can't function to its full potential.

5. Verses 6–8 indicate that each of us possesses gifts. While this passage is referring to spiritual gifts given by the Holy Spirit to be used for the benefit of the entire body, it is also true that every person has natural gifts, talents, and abilities.

6. Because of a misunderstanding of Christian humility, we are often discouraged from mentioning or even acknowledging our gifts and abilities. Yet every gift comes from God, given to us to use for his glory. Remind women in your group that gifts include much more than obvious talents in areas like music, athletics, academics, or art. A sympathetic listener is also gifted, as is the person who patiently and wisely raises her children. Encourage each group member to name her gifts and abilities. If someone is unable to think of anything, others in the group may help by indicating how they see that person. (Example: "You're always so cheerful, Mary. I feel better just being around you.")

7. Encourage everyone to share. If someone can't think of ways to use her abilities for the Lord, others in the group may suggest ideas.

8. Feelings of worthiness are supported and strengthened by the loving relationships we develop with other people. They bring meaning, purpose, and fulfillment into our lives. Jesus himself is the perfect example of this. How he loved and supported his disciples! And he expected them to follow his leading. " 'A new command I give you: Love one another,' " he said. "As I have loved you, so you must love one another. By this all men will know that you are my disciples, if you love one another' " (John 13:34–35). If you have time at this point in the lesson, you may want to expand this discussion with an examination of the characteristics of love found in 1 Corinthians 13.

9. Love for oneself is inseparably intertwined with love for God and others.

10. All of the statements are true. Allow time to discuss each statement and any insights gained from working through them.

11. Saying we love each other isn't enough. We are told to love each other completely, not only in word but also in actions (1 John 3:18). Our actions prove our love.

IV. Encourage group members to think in specifics. Discuss possible ways to show love to other people.

Conclude this first lesson by reminding your group members that regardless of past circumstances, it is possible to feel truly worthwhile. Because of his unconditional love for us, God can transform any woman into the whole, emotionally healthy person he wants her to be.

2 / BEAUTY, INTELLIGENCE, AND WEALTH

I. For the opening activity, you'll need magazines, scissors, glue, and a piece of poster board.

When the collage is completed, encourage each group member to share in the discussion. Most likely the characteristics represented in the collage will be physical attractiveness and accumulated possessions. Many women will see no similarity between themselves and "The Ideal American Woman."

II. Statements *A, B, D,* and *E* are true. Statement *C* is false.

1. Encourage group members to give their reasons for agreement or disagreement.

2. We are influenced by all the sources quoted—and more. Just how strongly each woman is affected by each will vary.

III. 1. a. Samuel's assignment was to anoint the man whom God had chosen to be king.

b. When he saw Eliab, Samuel thought: *he's tall, he's strong, he's handsome. Surely he's the one God has chosen to be the next king.*

c. After Samuel had seen seven of Jesse's sons, Samuel said: "Are these all the sons you have?"

2. Since the Bible doesn't tell us how each of these people felt about David, there can be no right or wrong answers here. Encourage each group member to share her ideas and the reasons for them.

3. Again, this question asks for a personal opinion. You may want to suggest the last section of verse 7 as a key verse: "Man looks at the outward appearance, but the Lord looks at the heart." This should encourage anyone whose heart is right with God.

IV. 1. Because physical attributes, social position, intellect, and wealth are so much a part of our society's value system, many women may have listed them. Inward characteristics and one's relationship with God probably will have been listed less often.

2. Instruct the women to base their analysis on what they have written in the boxes.

3. Encourage them to consider all the ideas in the lesson as they decide what changes they will want to make.

3 / THE ONLY TRUE VALUES

I. After the figures are filled in, allow time for each group member to discuss her thoughts. Question 2 is a personal question, which need not be shared.

II. Give each group member opportunity to tell where on the line she placed her *X* and how she decided on that position. All three statements are absolutely true.

III. 1. Your group members will come up with a variety of ideas. Here are some suggestions:

Act justly—honesty, fairness with others, treating others as you would want to be treated, impartiality, living within the law.

Love mercy—forgiveness, generosity, compassion, leniency, concern, willingness to go the extra mile.

Walk humbly with your God—obedience to God, godliness, reverence toward God, servant's attitude, avoiding pride or arrogance.

2. The characteristics God values are: love for God, obedience to God, development of a personal relationship to God, love for others, humble spirit, respect for authority.

3. The statement is absolutely true.

IV. Encourage the group members to be as honest as they can. The ratings are for their consideration and should not be shared with the group.

1. Improving your relationship with God will strengthen your self-esteem, for it is through a correct understanding of your standing with God that you can be assured of your infinite value.

2. Encourage the group members to share their ideas about developing a closer relationship with God. These ideas may include: daily Scripture reading, daily prayer, fellowship with other believers, and consistent worship with a body of believers.

V. After a time of silent prayer, encourage as many women as are willing to pray aloud. Don't go around the circle or use any other systematic way that might make someone uncomfortable. Remind women that it is encouraging to hear others pray but that God hears silent prayers as clearly as he does spoken prayers. The silence between spoken prayers need not be awkward. Encourage the women to use these times to pray silently.

4 / SEEING YOURSELF THROUGH GOD'S EYES

I. Have an envelope and sheets of paper ready for each woman; give each woman one sheet for each of the other group members, plus five extra sheets. (Example: If your group has eight women, give each woman one envelope with twelve slips of paper—seven slips to fill out for the other group members and five slips to fill out later.)

If you feel it is needed, you might give some suggestions of qualities to look for: encourager, faithful friend, dependable in prayer, cheerful, concerned about others.

1. If some group members seem reluctant to share expressions of their own qualities, urge them to do so. Remind them that there is nothing wrong in accepting compliments.

2. Ask each woman to share not only how she felt about the sheets she received but also why she felt that way.

II. 1–6. Encourage each group member to dig deeply into her feelings for an accurate expression to complete each "I feel" statement.

7. As group members share theirs answers to this statement, guide them toward understanding two things: first, that God sees each of us as a precious creation, made in his own image; and second, that he loves each of us.

III. 1. a. David says we can't hide from God. Wherever we are—alone or in public, in darkness or in light—God sees all our deeds.

b. David believes that it was God who put him together before he was born.

c. David asserts that even before his birth, God knew exactly who and what David would be.

d. David believes that God knew everything that would happen every day of his life, even before David was born.

2. a. You were made in God's image (Gen. 1:27).

b. You were not redeemed with perishable things like silver and gold but with the precious blood of Christ (1 Peter 1:18).

c. God wants to give you all things (Rom. 8:32).

d. God wants to adopt you, to make you his children, joint heirs with Christ (Rom. 8:15–17).

e. He has prepared a place for you, and he will come back and take you with him so that you can be where he is (John 14:1–3).

IV. Have your group members read all the verses before they choose one. When everyone has chosen, ask each woman to read her selection and to explain what drew her to that verse. Encourage each group member to memorize her particular verse as a source of encouragement and reassurance.

5 / KNOW YOURSELF

I. You may want to begin this session by discussing the example and talking about ways in which this situation might be acted out. For instance, the person might show appreciation for the time spent on the gift rather than its beauty; or the person might emphasize the giver's thoughtfulness in making the gift herself. Expressions like "How thoughtful of you, Mary!" or "What a lot of time it must have taken you to make this, Mary. Thank you so much," show honest kindness to the giver. Honesty need not exclude kindness.

II. 1. The true/false answers will largely depend on each person's own thoughts. But you might guide the women to consider:

- Everyone is a sinner.
- Although someone else's sinfulness is not always apparent, no one is perfect.
- God knows everything, including your love for him.
- Every one of us was created by God in his image.
- Everyone has abilities and talents. Some are more obvious than others, some more impressive, but all are equally worthwhile. God wants us to use each one.
- God made each person the way he wants her to be.

To be dissatisfied with your actions can spur you on to improve yourself. But to feel you are hopeless because of who or what you are is to pass judgment on God's handiwork. Becoming the person God wants us to be involves self-improvement and self-acceptance.

2. Even though some of your group members may find it difficult to answer these questions, encourage them to do their best. Remind them that they don't need to share their answers unless they choose to.

III. 1. Carry each other's burdens.

2. If you think you are something when you are nothing, you deceive yourself.

3. Test your own actions. Then you can take pride in yourself, without comparing yourself to somebody else.

IV. 1. Ask the group members to share the ideas they listed in the boxes. Encourage them to be specific. If someone suggests "Love others," ask, "Is there someone you find especially hard to love?" If someone says "Be joyful," ask, "What are some specific ways of expressing joy?"

2. Encourage the women not only to share but also to incorporate each other's ideas. Remind them that one value of sharing ideas is to help each woman expand her ability to apply God's Word to her own life.

3–6. This is a personal inventory, not one to be shared.

V. Encourage several women to pray, perhaps one for each of the suggestions listed.

6 / BE CRITICAL, BE KIND

I. Allow time for group members to share one or more of their responses to the "I am" sentence completions.

II. Discuss the difference between realistic and unrealistic goals. Talk about how to set realistic goals. For example, to say, "I will never again lose my temper" is unrealistic. But to say, "When I feel myself getting angry, I'll remove myself from the situation and ask God to help me handle myself" is a realistic goal.

Some women may check "I should do more" in each area; others may not. Emphasize that it is also important to recognize that we have areas of strengths. Allow time for any who wish to share their personal areas of needed improvement and their own specific goals to do so.

III. 1. The answers to the statements are:

    a. false

    b. false

    c. true

    d. true

    e. false

    f. true

    g. true

    h. false

IV. Encourage group members to explain their answers to the three multiple-choice questions in this section. Some women may have circled more than one answer per question. For instance, it would be possible to feel burdened by a family member—feeling obligated to watch over her and at the same time feeling grateful for her willingness to help.

Stress that whoever a person is and whatever her strengths and weaknesses, God can accomplish his perfect plan through her life.

V. Ask group members to answer the self-evaluation

carefully and thoughtfully. Allow time for women to share their answers, but be careful not to pressure anyone.

VI. Suggest memorizing Philippians 4:8, either as a group or individually.

7 / IS IT REALLY OK TO LOVE MYSELF?

I. Allow time for group members to read the story of Claire's dinner party.

1. Certainly there was nothing wrong with Claire's recognizing and using her abilities. She should use them.

2. She was using it for her own good, to advance her husband's standing in his boss's eyes.

3. Although several of the words listed could describe Claire, the one that *best* describes her is "selfish."

4. We probably would have advised Claire to use her talent as a hostess to make Marian and her husband feel welcome and important.

II. 1. Although the women may have different answers, the best definition of loving oneself as we are using it in this lesson is c: understanding that God knew what he was doing when he loved me enough to send his Son to die for me.

2–5. Discuss each point on the chart. After the women have filled in the questions following the chart, discuss each question. If some women are still bothered by self-love, suggest other words to substitute for that term. Some possibilities might be "valuing yourself" or "respecting yourself."

III. 1. We are to love the Lord with all our heart, soul, mind, and strength.

2. Your group will certainly come up with various definitions. Some possibilities are:

Heart   means emotions, passion, adoration.

Soul   means spirit, life, consciousness, essence, faith.

Mind   means intellect, understanding, mental capacity, attitude.

Strength means determination to prove your love, zeal, intensity, enthusiasm.

3. How much you love yourself.

IV. The statements that help explain what it means to love your neighbor as yourself are: Healthy self-esteem is important; if you don't think much of yourself, you won't think much of your neighbor either; when God made you, he liked what he saw; the way you treat others shows what you think of yourself; you won't love others if you don't love yourself; your love for God is the basis of love in your life.

1. Jesus sums up all the commandments in two basic relationships: Your love for God—you are to love him with your entire being; and your love for your neighbor—you are to love her or him as you love yourself.

2. This indicates that far from being the sin we often think it to be, love for ourselves follows our love for God and precedes our ability to love others.

V. Encourage your group members to fill in the prayer chains with words and phrases that describe their own feelings. Allow time for each group member to formulate and pray a prayer from her prayer chain.

8 / SINFUL PRIDE OR CHRISTIAN HUMILITY?

I. For today's beginning activity, have available several old magazines, scissors, and two sheets of poster board or large sheets of paper. On one sheet print "HOLLY HUMBLE"; on the other print "PATRICIA PROUD." As the group members look for appropriate pictures, ask them to think of descriptive words and phrases to add to the sheets.

1–3. Discuss the group members' responses to these questions.

II. Group members will have different reactions to the idea of thinking so much about themselves. However they answer this question, encourage them to express their feelings freely. Urge them to be open to changing their opinions as they progress through this lesson.

1–2. Discuss definitions of humility and self-love.

III. 1. Students should *agree* that Christ had a high position with God, that he took a position low in status but high in worth, that he was obedient even to death, and that he was exalted after his death. Students should *disagree* that Christ talked about being inferior, that he was uncertain of his value as a person, and that he needed to flaunt his strengths.

2. Humility and fame or great success certainly can mix, but it must be on the Lord's terms. James tells us, "Humble yourselves before the Lord, and he will lift you up" (James 4:10).

IV. The chart can be completed in a variety of ways. The following will give you an idea of one approach. (The columns for *Me* and *Comments* are not included since they will be different for each person.) The columns *Me* and *Followers of Christ* will probably contain answers like "sometimes" or "usually." Encourage group members to give examples of when the characteristics are displayed and when they are not. Urge each member to share her answers and comments with the group.

	Christ	Followers of Christ
is proud		sometimes
focuses on success		sometimes
feels inferior		sometimes
needs to advertise strengths		sometimes
underestimates self		sometimes
overestimates self		sometimes
focuses on weakness		sometimes
focuses on abilities	XX	sometimes
recognizes need of God	XX	XX
is willing to use abilities to help others	XX	XX
displays false humility		
submits to God's will	XX	XX

	Christ	Followers of Christ
demands respect	XX	sometimes
does things God's way	XX	sometimes
does what seems right in own eyes		sometimes
demands rights		
gives up rights for higher cause	XX	sometimes
is willing to be trampled by others		
is a person of principle	XX	XX
is weak		
loves others as self	XX	sometimes
is conceited		
hates self		
respects self	XX	XX
is passive		
is strong	XX	sometimes

	Christ	Followers of Christ
elevates self above others		sometimes
places self below others		

1. The following is one possible summarization of the characteristics of each. Other ideas may be shared.

Christ was secure in who he was and in the nature of his mission here on earth. He had no need to insist on raising himself up, but neither did he push himself down.

Followers of Christ basically understood their standing before God. They attempted to follow the example Christ set for them. But they were not always consistent. In example after example, we see ourselves in their various struggles, successes, and failures.

Yourself: Each person will summarize herself differently. Encourage your group to see themselves as honestly as possible, neither minimizing nor accentuating their strengths and weaknesses.

V. This is a personal question and is not to be shared.
VI. Remind your group members that the point is not how much we are like Christ but how *willing* we are to model our lives after his example.

9 / GET RID OF YOUR GUILT

I. After all the women have written their responses to the skits, discuss the responses.

1. Linda's line of questioning probably will cause Kris to feel defensive and possibly guilty. Some may suggest she also feels justified.

3. Jan certainly felt justified in her actions.

4. Too often, either intentionally or unintentionally, prayer sessions can degenerate into gossip sessions. Remind your group members that it isn't necessary, or even advisable, to share details in order to pray effectively. Knowing there is a need is all that's necessary. God knows the details.

II. Some possible ways to complete these sentences include:

1. Guilt means to be worthy of blame, deserving of punishment.

2. Guilt is good when it points out areas that need to be changed, sins that need to be forgiven.

3. Guilt is bad when it keeps us crippled with feelings of being evil or deserving punishment even after God has forgiven us. It's also bad when it causes us to feel deserving of blame for things that fall under human rules rather than God's laws.

III.

CHRISTIANS	NON-CHRISTIANS
no condemnation	condemned by sin
set free from the law of sin and death	minds set on desires of sinful nature
righteous requirements of the law fully met	mind of sinful man is death
minds set on what the Spirit desires	doesn't/can't submit to God's law
mind controlled by the Spirit is life and peace	can't please God
spirit lives on	doesn't belong to Christ

will live again after death   hostile to God

IV. 1. Encourage discussion of the personal meaning of the verses listed.

2. The answers to the statements are:

a. God doesn't care if I sin—disagree.

b. God no longer holds my sins against me—agree. (Be sure to point out that this is true only of a person who has confessed her sins and asked God for forgiveness. Anyone who has not done so still carries the consequences of her sin.)

c. Some of my sins are unforgivable—disagree. (The only unforgivable sin is the sin of final rejection of Jesus Christ as one's personal Savior. Any other sin, however bad, can be forgiven simply by confessing the sin, repenting of it, and trusting Christ to grant forgiveness [1 John 1:9].)

d. God can forgive my sins—agree.

e. I have received God's forgiveness—this is a personal response.

f. I can regard myself as guiltless—anyone who has received God's forgiveness is guiltless in the eyes of God (Ps. 103:12).

g. Freedom from guilt means I can go on sinning—disagree (see Rom. 6:1–2).

V. Encourage each member to participate in the guided silent prayer and in the joyful reading of Romans 8:31–39.

10 / GOD HAS GREAT PLANS FOR YOU

I. For the game "Would You Rather?" divide the room into side A and side B. Then read out loud each set of choices and allow time for each group member to move to the side that indicates her choice.

Example: "Would you rather get a new pet or get rid of the one you have? If you would rather get a new pet, move to side A. If you would rather get rid of the one you have, move to side B."

II. After the group has responded to the "test cases," take time to discuss them. Rather than going through the entire list, you might ask questions like: In which areas are you most likely to fall apart? In which do you feel most together? Give an example of an area in which you are working to improve yourself. In which area can we help you think of ways to move toward "all together"?

III. 1. Moses was amazed to see the bush (c) on fire but not burning up.

2. God told Moses not to come any closer because (b) he was on holy ground.

3. God told Moses to (a) go to Pharoah and lead the Israelites out of Egypt.

4. As for convincing the Egyptians, (c) God would take care of it.

5. When Moses said he was not a gifted speaker, God said (c) he would help Moses speak and would teach him what to say.

IV. 1. Ask your group members to explain the emotions they think Moses felt.

2. Now ask them to share the emotions they feel when they are faced with a job that seems too big or impossible. Remind them that it is natural to feel weak, confused, frightened, etc. What is wrong is to allow our feelings to dominate and limit what we are willing to undertake. Encourage group members to describe times when they have gone against their fears and self-doubts and have been able to accomplish things they thought were impossible.

V. Urge each group member to record what she feels God wants her to do. Then encourage people to share their statements with the group. This may be too personal for some women, but remind them that it helps to have a group, or at least one or two people, to whom they can be accountable. Other people will be able to offer encouragement and to serve as reminders of God's purposes.

As each woman shares, jot down her name and a word or phrase to remind you of what she said. When everyone has had an opportunity to share, ask for a volunteer to pray specifically for each one who shared (the volunteer may want to use your list). Encourage those who didn't share to ask one or two friends to pray with them about the job they feel God has for them.

11 / SELF-LOVE SURRENDERED

I. You may want to think ahead of your own comments for each person in your group.

II. Surrendering your self-love to God will result in all of the things listed. (Some women may prefer to stress "I will *use* my gifts and abilities" rather than "I will *enjoy* my gifts and abilities.") Invite women to share their responses to the two remaining questions in this section. These questions will elicit opinions rather than right or wrong answers.

III. Your group members will fill in the chart in a variety of ways. These are suggested responses. *In verse 10,* love means being willing to sacrifice one's greatest treasure to save another, as demonstrated in God's sacrifice of his Son for us. *In verse 11,* love means reciprocation; we love each other as God first loved us. *In verse 20,* love means demonstrating our love for God by loving others. *In verse 21,* love means obeying God's command to love each other.

1. The two love relationships are: God's love for us and our love for God as demonstrated by our love for others.

2. This means God already loves me; Jesus died to atone for my sins; I love because God first loved me; if I love God, I will love others; if I love only myself, it will show in the way I relate to others.

IV. 1. The descriptive words may include these:

God's love is sacrificial, perfect, undeserved, endless, the foundation of all other love.

Self-love results from God's love for me, enables me to love others, is demonstrated by my love for others, is a healthy love.

Love for others is modeled after God's love, results from God's love for me, proves my love for God, is God's command to me, is a natural outgrowth of self-love.

2. These sentences can be completed in a variety of ways. Invite the women to share their responses. Some responses may include ideas like:

a. I can love God when I'm sick by trusting his love for me and his promise to work all things together for my good. I can continue to pray for healing, but I will not demand my own way. I can show my love for him by trusting that he is wiser than I am and that his ways are right.

b. I can love an abusive or violent family member by trying to get professional help for that person. I can insist that the person take responsibility for his or her behavior. I can show love by forgiving that person for the abusive behavior. I can pray for that person.

c. I can love a friend who has taken advantage of me by forgiving that person and by returning good for evil. I can show love by refusing to take revenge and by praying for him or her.

d. I can show love to a needy person by giving time and money to agencies and groups that help the needy. I can choose not to be judgmental toward those in difficulty. And I can show love by asking God to bring to me those people whom I can help.

V. Encourage the women in your group to pray by name for one or two people on their family love tree. Encourage them to commit themselves to become channels through which God's love can flow to these people.

12 / A HEALTHY SELF-CONCEPT AT WORK

I. Have stickers or pieces of candy available for the game of "Give Away." You will also need a die. Following the chart, play the game until one player is out of stickers or candy. When the game is over, discuss the questions.

II. These are suggested answers. Give opportunity for people with differing opinions to explain their answers.

Forgiving others—Eph. 4:32b; 1 Peter 2:1; Rom. 12:19.

Showing generosity—Eph. 4:32a; James 1:27; Heb. 13:5; Luke 6:38; Acts 20:35; 2 Cor. 9:7.

Honoring others—Prov. 1:22; 1 Peter 2:1; Eph. 4:32a; Eph. 4:26; Eph. 5:21; Rom. 12:10; 1 John 4:21; Phil. 2:13.

Being grateful—1 Thess. 5:18; 2 Cor. 9:15; Col. 3:15.

III. 1. The gifts listed in these verses include wisdom, knowledge, faith, the gift of healing, miraculous powers, prophecy, ability to distinguish between spirits, ability to speak in different kinds of tongues, and the interpretation of tongues.

2. No one gift is more important than any other.

3. The Holy Spirit gives them as he sees fit.

4. Every member of the body receives one or more gifts.

5. Paul didn't want the Corinthians to be ignorant of the gifts they had been given.

6. This is a personal question that need not be discussed.

IV. Allow plenty of time to discuss this section. Try to motivate each group member to share both her need of the gifts of others and ways in which she can use her gifts for the good of others. Emphasize the point that both giving and receiving are important.

V. Discuss the list of ways to boost the self-esteem of those around you. Encourage your group members to add their own ideas to the list.

Urge each woman to commit herself to praying for one other person.

13 / LOOKING TOWARD YOUR ULTIMATE SELF

I. Have available magazines, scissors, and glue. Encourage the women to fill in the circles with a variety of expressions: words, pictures, verses, and phrases.

2. Allow time for everyone to share, but don't press anyone who may be reluctant. Discuss one circle at a time and ask for volunteers to share.

II. Encourage women to concentrate on the future, on the unlimited opportunities they have as they move ahead in the power of the Lord. Encourage them to pray specifically for characteristics they want to see developing in themselves:

forgiveness, hope, assurance, encouragement, peace, patience, etc.

III. 1. Because God loves us so much, he calls us <u>his children</u>.

2. The reason the world does not know us is that <u>it did not know him</u>.

3. When Christ returns, we will <u>be like him</u>, for we shall <u>see him as he is</u>.

4. Regardless of how wonderful it is to be assured you are special and worthwhile now, it can't be compared with the joys you will know when <u>he returns and takes you to heaven to live with him forever</u>!

5–6. Take time to discuss the promises for the future and what they mean to the women in your group.

IV. The readers of John's letters may have felt encouraged, mystified, excited, relieved, and filled with hope.

1. Invite members to share their feelings. Remind them that passages like 1 John 3 are to encourage us and fill us with hope, not to frighten or confuse us.

2. Be sure each group member understands that it's possible for her to know without any doubt that she will live forever with the Lord. Remind the group that Jesus is ready and waiting. Each person needs only to accept his offer of forgiveness and salvation through his sacrificial death on the cross and his resurrection. If anyone is not sure she has taken this step, urge her to come to the Lord and ask him for his free gift of salvation. (See verses like John 3:16–18; 1 John 1:8–9; and Romans 8:1.)

V. Invite several volunteers to share the last evaluation. Close with a session of thanksgiving prayer, allowing time for many to thank the Lord for his love, his forgiveness, and the assurance he provides of eternal life with him.

Read together with your group the Steps for Attaining Healthy Self-Esteem, found on the page following lesson 13.